JESUS #NOFILTER

WHEN JESUS' WORDS OFFEND YOU

BY MIKE NOVOTNY

Published by Straight Talk Books
P.O. Box 301, Milwaukee, WI 53201
800.661.3311 • timeofgrace.org

Printed in the United States of America
ISBN: 978-1-949488-87-6

CONTENTS

Introduction
5

You Need Jesus
The Bread of Life
11

Without Jesus, There's Only Darkness
The LIGHT of the World
25

No One Can Keep You Safe Like Jesus
The Good Shepherd
37

Only Jesus' Voice Shows the Way
The Gate
51

Connected to Jesus, You Will Grow
The Vine
63

Jesus Is the ONLY Way to Heaven
The Way, the Truth, and the Life
77

Jesus Means Life After Death for You
The Resurrection and the Life
91

Conclusion
103

INTRODUCTION

When I was kid, about 9 in 10 Americans claimed to be Christian. Now, according to the Pew Research Center, about 6 in 10 Americans claim to be Christian.[1] If trends continue and I die an old man, less than 5 in 10 Americans will claim to be Christian. Why would that be?

Let's make it more personal. Why, perhaps, did your grandma and grandpa go to church but now one or two or more than a few of the grandkids do not? Why were your siblings raised with religion but now a couple want nothing to do with it? Or why will some of the people reading this book not go to church anymore next year?

There are a lot of answers to that question, I suppose—from church hypocrisy to man-made rules to church services that don't make sense and seem to have nothing to do with real life. But I think there is one answer that explains a lot of what is happening right now in America: *the unfiltered Jesus is offensive.*

Unfiltered. Think of a filter for a second. A filter turns *what is* into *what you want it to be.* For example, a coffee or a car or a furnace filter turns what something is into what you want it to be. When you make coffee, you want flavored water, not gritty grounds, so you use a filter. You don't want all the junk in the air getting into your car engine, so you use a filter. Or think of a filtered picture. You take what is (your face) and turn it into what you want it to be (blemishes gone; Snapchat funny face on). Filters take what actually is and turn it into what you want it to be.

That's interesting when you think of Jesus. Sooner or later, if you read everything Jesus said in the Bible, you'll be offended. Jesus will call you out or tell you to change your mind or insist that your friends are wrong even though they think they're right. When that happens, and it normally happens through a human who is just quoting what Jesus said, it is a massive spiritual moment. Will you try to filter Jesus' teaching so he says what you want? Will you just give up altogether? Will you stay even though you're offended? Likely, that moment has already happened or will soon happen to your brother or your best friend or the guy you're with or you.

As you read this book, I'd like you to think about those questions. Because in chapter after chapter, I will quote the Bible book of John, where Jesus makes many claims about himself—claims that he backed up with authoritative teaching and miracles of many kinds, including raising people from the dead. The heavenly Father claimed him as his Son (Matthew 3:16,17; 17:5). He is the Son of God—true man and true God. He claimed to bring life, light, mercy, and salvation to us. As you read what Jesus says about himself, will it turn you away from him or toward him? Will you try to filter him and what he says to fit your idea of him or your interpretation of his words? Will you change his words so they are more in line with what you want to believe? It's my prayer that the Holy Spirit will lead you to believe that the unfiltered Jesus is worthy of your praise. Yes, his teachings are hard at times, but they are also full of love. Grace and truth—that's the unfiltered Jesus. He's worth the criticism you might get for believing in him. He's worth the sacrifices you might need to make to follow him. He's worth it!

I AM THE BREAD OF LIFE. WHOEVER COMES TO ME WILL NEVER GO HUNGRY, AND WHOEVER BELIEVES IN ME WILL NEVER BE THIRSTY.

JOHN 6:35

YOU NEED JESUS

The Bread of Life

Will you try to filter Jesus' teaching so he says what you want? Will you stay even though you're offended? What happens when you're confronted with these questions after reading your Bible or when someone points out what Jesus says to you?

Let me tell you about a time it happened to five thousand people two thousand years ago. There was this moment when 99 percent of the people who loved Jesus started to hate him and when the other 1 percent struggled but still followed him. Today in a culture that is increasingly like the 99 percent, I want to tell you why the 1 percent stuck around.

Let's jump into John chapter 6 and the biggest numerical miracle Jesus ever did—the feeding of the five thousand. Soon after Jesus started to heal people with his divine power, the crowds started to gather. Dozens turned into hundreds, and hundreds turned into thousands who were interested in him. One day, five thousand men showed up (with possibly just as many women and children), turning Jesus into a megachurch pastor. Since no one was type A enough to plan and pack their own lunches, Jesus did a mega miracle. He took a little kid's brown-bag Lunchables and fed the entire crowd! And the people realized something stunning—Jesus was full of power and love. He had so much power that he could make food appear and sicknesses disappear. He had so much love that he wanted to do these things for people. Thus, the crowd decided to make Jesus their king, a unanimous vote for the brand-new king of the Jews.

But Jesus wasn't flattered. Soon after the miracle, he started to preach. John chapter 6 records:

> **Jesus answered, "Very truly I tell you, you are looking for me, not because you saw the signs I performed but because you ate the loaves and had your fill. Do not work for food that spoils, but for food that endures to eternal life, which the Son of Man will give you. For on him God the Father has placed his seal of approval."**
>
> **Then they asked him, "What must we do to do the works God requires?"**
>
> **Jesus answered, "The work of God is this: to believe in the one he has sent."** (verses 26-29)

"I can give you 'bread' from heaven, bread that satisfies you forever, food that fills you up and makes you live for all eternity," Jesus said.

The crowd was curious. "Something that lasts forever? And you're just giving it away? Give us that bread, Jesus!"

Jesus replied:

> **"I am the bread of life. Whoever comes to me will never go hungry, and whoever believes in me will never be thirsty. For I have come down from heaven not to do my will but to do the will of him who sent me."** (verses 35,38)

But that line was a bit . . . offensive. John continues:

> **At this the Jews there began to grumble about him because he said, "I am the bread that came down from heaven." They said, "Is this not Jesus, the son of Joseph, whose father and mother we know? How can he now say, 'I came down from heaven'?"** (verses 41,42)

"Jesus, come on. You're not from heaven. You're from earth, just like us. We know your parents. You didn't float down like some angel. You came out of your momma, Mary, born just like the rest of us. From heaven? Nah."

Why were they so offended? Because *the authoritative Jesus is offensive*. If Jesus is from heaven, that means he is higher than us. It means he knows God better than we do. It means he knows better than we do. And that claim didn't sit right with the crowd.

It still doesn't. Something in your heart and mine really hates authority, doesn't it? I really like the government—the freedoms, the structure, the safety—unless the government says I have to do something I don't want to do—25 mph? How much for taxes? Don't tell me how to live! Then I hate the government. I really like referees—they keep grown men from breaking my legs when I'm trying to score a goal—unless the referee says something I don't agree with. Then I hate referees. Kids often love their parents—parents pay the rent, buy the food, drive them to practice—that is, until the parents tell them to go to bed, clean their rooms, put away the phones. Then they hate them.

And we love Jesus—he's with us, loves us, has a plan for us—that is, unless he commands and demands and insists. We love him until he preaches about marriage and divorce, the wickedness of human nature, the fact that hell is full and heaven has room—the doctrine and dogma. Jesus preaches with the authority of heaven. He claims to be better than you, to know better than you, every single time. If you read the Bible and disagree, you are wrong. If someone confronts your behavior with an open Bible and you disagree, you are wrong. Because you are from earth and Jesus is from heaven.

Offended? They were too, but Jesus wasn't done:

> **"Stop grumbling among yourselves," Jesus answered. "I am the living bread that came down from heaven. Whoever eats this bread will live forever. This bread is my flesh, which I will give for the life of the world."**
>
> **Then the Jews began to argue sharply among themselves, "How can this man give us his flesh to eat?"**
>
> **Jesus said to them, "Very truly I tell you, unless you eat the flesh of the Son of Man and drink his blood, you have no life in you."** (verses 43,51-53)

Jesus chose an offensive image here. He hadn't invented the Lord's Supper yet, so this wasn't that. This was Jesus saying, "You need me. Unless you have me within you, unless you come to me, believe in me, 'eat and drink' me spiritually, you have no life in you." Here's the second thing the unfiltered Jesus claimed: *"I am essential."*

Think of Jesus' metaphor. Your body needs bread (or some kind of food). Needs it. You will die very quickly without it. Your body does not have the ability to produce the calories it needs to live. Your body requires something from the outside to save it, or it will die. Not just once or twice, but all the time. Your body needs bread. And Jesus said, "I am the Bread of Life." Your soul, like your body, does not have the ability to produce what it needs to live. To be with

God, you have to be really good, holy, sinless, pure. And we aren't. And we can't make ourselves that way from the inside out. Jesus was saying, "You need me. I am the Bread of Life. Without me, you can't have life with God. You will go to hell. But if you eat and drink, come to me and believe, you will live. You'll live with God forever."

That was too much for most everyone who heard it.

> **On hearing it, many of his disciples said, "This is a hard teaching. Who can accept it?" From this time many of his disciples turned back and no longer followed him.** (verses 60,66)

And just like that, Jesus' megachurch was over. The unfiltered Jesus was just too offensive.

So why would you follow Jesus? This is how Jesus is. He is the Lord who gets the last word. He never repents or says he's wrong, so what will you do with Jesus? Will you believe in him? You should. I was reminded why by a former addict recently.

A few months back, I wandered into a local toy collector's shop and struck up a conversation with "Rick," the owner. I used to be huge into sports cards, so we started exchanging stories about the most expensive cards we had ever owned. Rick shared that he had some rare Derek Jeter and Alex Rodriguez cards that now sell for thousands of dollars. "Whoa," I said. "Did you keep them?"

Rick smiled and shook his head, "No, I probably traded

them for a cheeseburger or some weed when I was high." He gave away something of immense value because he was just thinking about the moment.

Forgive my crass analogy, but giving away Jesus to do what you want is like paying thousands to smoke a joint. I've never done it, but I've heard that's a bad deal, because even in the midst of all the offensive things he said, Jesus was trying to remind the crowds that he was giving them something so much more. In fact, I read through his long message in John 6:25-59 and found Jesus offering these blessings: "I will give you food that endures to eternal life. God sent me for you! You will never go hungry! You will never be thirsty! I won't drive you away. I won't lose you. I will raise you up on the Last Day. You will have eternal life. I will teach you. You will live forever. You will live because of me. I have chosen you!" Think of that! Jesus wants you to live forever with God! Jesus wants to end your pain, struggles, stress, sickness, tension, issues. He came from heaven to save you, to satisfy you, to make sure that your 75 years on this earth are all the suffering you will ever do. He came to give you eternal life, eternal happiness, eternal rest, an eternity with God!

There's a logic to Jesus' message: "Yes, I am in authority over you. Yes, you are so sinful that you need me. But if you are humble enough to believe that, look at what I'm offering you! Don't be the four-year-old who runs away from a loving home just because he doesn't get to make his own bedtime! I'm offering you life! Life with God! Eternal life!"

There will come a time when Jesus offends you or when

a Christian pastor or Christian parent or Christian friend comes with a Bible and shows you that you are wrong and that you need to repent. They might even say that living your truth will cost you eternal life. When that moment comes, when you think about joining the thousands who walked away, remember what Peter said:

> **"You do not want to leave too, do you?" Jesus asked the Twelve.**
>
> **Simon Peter answered him, "Lord, to whom shall we go? You have the words of eternal life. We have come to believe and to know that you are the Holy One of God."** (verses 67-69)

Jesus is offering you the words of eternal life. Jesus, despite all your sins and all your shame, was sent from heaven for you. He will not turn you away. He will give everything he has to save you.

Here's my summary of John chapter 6: *Jesus is so offensive and so worth it.* A few people realized that. "Yeah, that was a hard sermon, Jesus, but we know who you are. We know what you're giving us. Where else could we go to find life with God?"

Jesus might cost you a lot, but he is the Bread of Life. Whoever eats this bread will live forever.

STUDY QUESTIONS

1. Read John 6:25–29 and evaluate the following statement: God often uses physical needs (accidents, cancer, financial stress, etc.) to bring us to Jesus, but he never wants us to follow Jesus for physical reasons.

2. Compare John 6:27; 6:35; and 4:13,14. What point did Jesus continually make when speaking with hungry and thirsty people? How might your answer change the way you pray this week?

3. John 6:47 reminds us (again) that we are saved through faith and not by doing enough good things for God. List at least five blessings that this truth gives you. (For example—The gift of salvation frees me from the fear that I haven't done enough good to make it to heaven.)

4. The Bible describes how the number of Jesus' followers grew from his bold and faithful preaching (see John 3:26) and also how the number shrank (see John 6:66). Why is this so important for modern churches to remember, especially in an American culture that is obsessed with data, growth, and the belief that bigger is better?

5. Ponder Peter's words in John 6:68 and fill in this sentence in as many ways as possible: "Jesus, to whom shall I go? You have ___________."

I AM THE LIGHT
OF THE WORLD.
WHOEVER FOLLOWS
ME WILL NEVER
WALK IN DARKNESS,
BUT WILL HAVE THE
LIGHT OF LIFE.

JOHN 8:12

WITHOUT JESUS, THERE'S ONLY DARKNESS

The LIGHT of the World

In early 2023, two sports commentators with very different beliefs both claimed they believed in the unfiltered Jesus. On the one side was Super Bowl champion coach and NFL analyst Tony Dungy. On the other was *USA Today* columnist Nancy Armour. The debate over Jesus started after Tony apologized for a recent tweet about transgender people that he admitted was not fitting for a follower of Jesus. Nancy responded with an entire article about Dungy, accusing him of way more than an unchristian tweet but instead of holding unchristian beliefs. She wrote, "If you are Christian, you are supposed to follow the teachings of Christ. . . . [Christ] preached love and acceptance, embracing lepers, prostitutes and the hated tax collectors, and had no use for those who proclaimed their piety while using it to demean and mistreat others."[2] Tony and Nancy hold two very different positions on these very important issues, but both claim to be following Jesus' example.

Whose side is Jesus on? Behind most of the fiercest moral debates of our time is the idea that Jesus is on *my* side. Was Jesus against organized religion or the founder of an organized religion? Did Jesus stand up for the rules of religion, or did he stand with the outcasts who had broken the rules? Did he tell his followers to judge others or just to love others? Are we called to call out injustice and sin and every evil or just to love our neighbor as much as we love ourselves? What would Jesus do? What would Jesus tell us to do?

There is only one good way to answer these questions—the unfiltered Jesus. Filters are things that change what something really is into what we want it to be. But if we don't filter out Jesus, if we just listen to everything he said, we can get the real thing. The real Christ. Real Christianity. Jesus is going to help us do just that.

John 8:12 says, **"When Jesus spoke again to the people, he said, 'I am the light of the world. Whoever follows me will never walk in darkness, but will have the light of life.'"** Jesus is the Light. When you stop and really think about light, you can learn a lot about the identity of Jesus. In fact, I had a chance to read all 398 Bible passages that mentioned "light" or "dark" or "darkness," and I was able to fit their meaning into the acronym LIGHT. Now—full disclosure—it's not the best acronym ever. If there was an award show for Acronym of the Year (the Acron-emmys?), I wouldn't win. I wouldn't even be nominated. But I do hope LIGHT helps you understand and adore who the real Jesus really is.

The *L* stands for *life*. Jesus himself pointed to this in this verse when he said, "Whoever follows me . . . will have the light of life." Do you know how plants work? They live, in part, because of photosynthesis, which is where they soak in light that gives life to their cells. No light, no life. In fact, the few plants that seem to live in total darkness actually feed off other plants that have been in the light! They need light to live!

We do too. You can't have spiritual life or eternal life or life with God at all without Jesus, which is what he claimed in our last chapter: "I am the Bread of Life." He is essential for your soul like bread is for your body. While you could see these words as controversial, I find them a great comfort. Whoever follows Jesus has life. "Whoever" includes you. Even if you've done *that*. Even if you still feel guilty about saying *that*. Jesus isn't offering life to the really good people or the saints who may appear to have never sinned. He's offering life to you. He is the Light of the world, and the world includes you. That means Jesus is giving you, through faith in him, eternal life with God.

Second, the *I* in LIGHT stands for *I see*. Because when the lights are on, I see. I see a chair, my desk, a thousand things I couldn't identify in the dark. When we really see the truth of something, we call it enlightenment. Since Jesus is the Light of the world, he enlightens us and lets us see what is true.

A few years ago, my wife, Kim, and I almost became prey to some giant predators in northern Thailand. I was there to speak to some missionaries, and our hotel was in this huge complex that had a park and a zoo and paths all around. We got up when it was still dark to run. When I say dark, I mean really dark. And that's when two predators stopped us in our tracks! We could barely see where the path was. Suddenly we looked up and saw two huge beasts with their ears sticking straight up in the darkness! We gasped and panicked and ran the other direction (if you're wondering if we died, we didn't). When sunlight broke, we went back to the scene and saw . . . two giant shrubbery bunnies. Turns out our hotel had a topiary garden, which is where they trim bushes into shapes such as bunnies. That's right. I thought I was about to be eaten alive by a shrub! I thought it was a predator.

You and I think lots of untrue things in the dark. But Jesus is the Light. Jesus helps us see what's true. Read the words of Jesus, and you won't have to guess about life's greatest questions: Who are you? Who is God? What happens after you die? What's your purpose right now? Listen to Jesus, and you'll see: You and I are sinners saved by grace. God is the most glorious, wonderful, powerful, loving Father. When we die, Jesus takes us to heaven. For now, we love God by obeying his commandments and by loving our neighbors.

Want to know the truth about your life? Follow Jesus, and you will have the light of life.

Next, the G stands for *growth*. Plants don't just live because of the light; they grow in the light. Their cells grow and then divide, which makes plants bigger and stronger. Their growth and their strength are connected to light. That's true for your mental health too, isn't it? If you battle depression, it's tempting to stay in the dark. You don't want to get out of bed, but it's essential to get into the light. Fresh air and warm sun are ingredients for a strong mind.

Jesus does the same thing for your soul. You wake up and grab his Word because you want to grow. You want his strength for the day ahead. You want Jesus to remind you of the life you have with God, to help you see the world from his point of view, and to grow in your amazement of God's love. Do you set aside time in your day to soak in the light of his Word? If not, today is the best day to start. I know it won't glow when you open it, but the Bible contains the light. Actually, if you have a Bible app, it will glow! Either way, you'll get God, grace, and growth, because Jesus is the Light of the world.

I just met a guy from our church who is exploding with spiritual growth. He's pretty new to all this, but he is experiencing a spiritual growth spurt that everyone in his life sees. I asked him about his Bible habits, and he told me about his "holy hour," the first hour of his day when he reads the Bible or listens to sermons and takes notes on what Jesus is saying. He's growing. That's not surprising. Because light is the source of growth.

Then there's the *H*. The *H* in LIGHT stands for *harsh*.

Light can be harsh. Have your parents ever busted into your bedroom to wake you up for school and flipped on the lights? Harsh. Has anyone ever shined a flashlight in your face? Harsh. Ever stepped out into a bright day without sunglasses? Harsh. When I was growing up, Abercrombie & Fitch kept the lights real low in their dressing rooms. We all looked a bit better in the dark.

If Jesus is the Light, that means he can be harsh. His teaching can expose us and make us want to hide under the covers. Jesus himself admitted this earlier in John's gospel: **"This is the verdict: Light has come into the world, but people loved darkness instead of light because their deeds were evil. Everyone who does evil hates the light, and will not come into the light for fear that their deeds will be exposed"** (3:19,20). Why didn't everyone love Jesus? Because he was the Light who exposed the sins of men. The unfiltered Jesus can be harsh.

And he'll shine a light on you too. If you want to live your truth, follow your heart, claim autonomy and authority over your body, and think that going to church means you don't have to change, you're gonna hate Jesus. Because Jesus points his Word like a helicopter spotlight on your heart and says, "That's wrong." Thinking it's okay because you feel it? No. That's wrong. Going to church and then being a jerk? Um, no. That has to change. You can run from the light and back to the dark, you can avoid the harsh truth that calls you to repent, but then there will be no life, no sight, no growth, no God.

I hope you don't, because Jesus is your *safeTy*. Okay, I

know that's cheating with the acronym, but I couldn't find a word that started with *T* that seemed to fit. The dark is dangerous. You can run into things. You can get hurt. But in the light, you stay safe. Jesus said, **"I am the light of the world. Whoever follows me will never walk in darkness"** (John 8:12). This is a stunning promise. If you follow Jesus—if you repent of your sins and trust in him—you will never walk in darkness. That means you will never be in danger of going to hell. Never in danger of missing heaven. Never in danger of being alone or unloved or lost. Never not forgiven. Never not on God's mind. Jesus saves you from all that danger, because Jesus is the Light of the world.

In fact, in the original Greek of the New Testament, Jesus put it more strongly. The word *never* could be translated "never, ever, ever!" If you have Jesus, you will never, ever, ever not be with God and his love and his forgiveness and his presence and his plans for you and his strength and his Spirit. Never, ever, ever.

And if you're a Bible nerd like me, you'll love that Jesus said this during the Jewish Feast of Tabernacles, a holiday to celebrate how God kept his people safe during all those years in the wilderness when he showed up as a pillar of fire (light!) so they wouldn't be alone or afraid. Jesus is saying, "I am that Light. I am God. And I will keep you safe until you get to the real Promised Land. The devil and every demon could march against you, but my blood will keep you safe. My sacrifice on a cross protects you from the danger of their shame. That's what I will do, because that is who I am."

That is what Jesus meant when he said that he is the LIGHT. Life with God. I see the truth. Growth in my faith. Harsh exposure of my sins. Safety from every spiritual danger. Want to know how people reacted to Jesus' unfiltered message? John says, **"The Pharisees challenged him. . . . Many believed in him"** (John 8:13,30). Some fought back. Some followed.

And you? Jesus is the Light of the world, but people follow one by one. Whoever follows Jesus will never, ever, ever live in darkness. So don't run from the Light. I know Jesus can be harsh. I know his teaching can be hard. But he and only he is the Light of the world and the Light of life.

In a world that is living in the dark, God wants to open your eyes today. The Holy Spirit wants to change your heart to turn you in another direction, to turn you toward Jesus. Not some cruel and ruthless Lord, but the Lord of light. The One whose love led him to a cross for the forgiveness of all the things you did in the dark. Follow Jesus, and you will never, ever, ever live without light.

STUDY QUESTIONS

1. Isaiah wrote a famous prophecy about Jesus in Isaiah 9:1–7. Meditate on these ancient words, underlining every phrase that reminds you of your Savior.

2. Read the start of John's gospel (John 1:1–9). What connections to LIGHT do you see in those verses?

3. Study Paul's words about light/darkness in Ephesians 5:8–14. Which words/phrases do you feel are most relevant to our modern culture?

4. Jesus once said to his disciples, "You are the light of the world" (Matthew 5:14). What did he mean by that? How does this apply to your group of Christian friends?

5. To bring light to this dark world, Christians must go out into the world. What does this statement say to Christians who prefer to be friends only with Christians, do business only with Christians, go to school only with Christians, and spend their free time only with Christians?

I AM THE
GOOD SHEPHERD.
THE GOOD SHEPHERD
LAYS DOWN HIS LIFE
FOR THE SHEEP.

JOHN 10:11

NO ONE CAN KEEP YOU SAFE LIKE JESUS

The Good Shepherd

Jesus is our Good Shepherd. Have you heard that before? If not, that's okay, but if you've spent any amount of time in the church, you've probably heard that metaphor before—Jesus is our Good Shepherd.

There are many churches named Good Shepherd. My daughter has a framed picture above her bed of Jesus holding a lamb like a loving shepherd. And in my church lobby, you'll see a wall mural with the name of Jesus and all his titles from the Bible, including Shepherd. And that's fitting, because that's exactly what Jesus said about himself: **"I am the good shepherd"** (John 10:11).

How do you feel about that metaphor? If you had to name your gut reaction, your emotional response, to Jesus' words, what would it be? That image of you and Jesus. You held in his strong arms. You wrapped around his shoulders as he carries you home. I'm not sure how you feel when you hear it, but I do know how the Jews in Jesus' day felt when they first heard it:

> **The Jews who heard these words were again divided. Many of them said, "He is demon-possessed and raving mad. Why listen to him?"**
>
> **But others said, "These are not the sayings of a man possessed by a demon."** (John 10:19–21)

"Good Shepherd? This dude is demon-possessed. This guy is nuts. I'm out. Unfollow."

But others disagreed, "No. Demons don't talk like this. What if he really is the Son of God?"

When you take off the filters and listen to the unedited, unadulterated, uncut words of Jesus, you can't shrug or yawn or say, "That's nice." No, that's not an option. Jesus forces you to take sides, to figure out what you believe about who he is. C. S. Lewis caught that. Lewis was an atheist who taught at Oxford and Cambridge and became a Christian in his early 30s after a long talk with his friend J. R. R. Tolkien (the guy who wrote *Lord of the Rings*). In one of his best quotes, Lewis later said this about the real Jesus:

> I am trying here to prevent anyone saying the really

> foolish thing that people often say about Him: "I'm ready to accept Jesus as a great moral teacher, but I don't accept His claim to be God." That is the one thing we must not say. A man who was merely a man and said the sort of things Jesus said would not be a great moral teacher. He would either be a lunatic . . . or else he would be the Devil of Hell. . . . Either this man was, and is, the Son of God: or else a madman or something worse. You can shut Him up for a fool, you can spit at Him and kill Him as a demon; or you can fall at His feet and call Him Lord and God. But let us not come with any patronizing nonsense about His being a great human teacher. He has not left that open to us. He did not intend to.[3]

And that is exactly what happened with the real Jesus. That's why I want to teach you about a familiar picture—the Good Shepherd—from a fresh angle. Based on the words of Jesus and the reaction of those who heard Jesus, here's this chapter's big idea: *Jesus is our Good Shepherd (no offense, and thank God!)*. As we take another look at the claims that Jesus made about himself in the gospel of John, I want to introduce you to the extremely offensive and absolutely amazing Jesus, our Good Shepherd.

> **"I am the good shepherd. The good shepherd lays down his life for the sheep. The hired hand is not the shepherd and does not own the sheep. So when**

he sees the wolf coming, he abandons the sheep and runs away. Then the wolf attacks the flock and scatters it. The man runs away because he is a hired hand and cares nothing for the sheep.

"I am the good shepherd." (John 10:11-14)

Offended? Maybe you weren't paying attention. Because Jesus used the word *shepherd* three times to talk about himself, and he used the word *sheep* four times to talk about you and me. No offense.

Think about sheep for a second. Sheep are pretty important creatures, producing wool, milk, cheese, meat, mattress stuffing, and the cover of tennis balls (thanks, sheep!). But sheep have two fatal flaws. First, they are prone to wander. Sheep stray and separate themselves from the shepherd. Why? In part, because they don't pay attention. They're grazing on some green grass right here and then see some more green grass over there and—oh!—there's more grass over there, and eventually they end up wandering far away from their shepherd. Plus, sheep are followers, and sometimes they will follow an alpha sheep who wanders. Their flocking instinct keeps them close to their friends, even if their friends are straying from the shepherd. That's the first flaw of being a sheep—they wander.

The second flaw is that when they wander, they end up in danger. Wolves. Short sheep legs can't stretch out like a cheetah. The wool, which can add double-digit pounds, weighs a sheep down. A varsity sheep can't outrun even a JV wolf. Just like your short uncle with his beer belly can't win the local 5K, sheep can't outrun their predators. And there are no wings or claws or fangs. So when a wolf comes, the sheep are in danger. Sheep can't save themselves. The sheep have wandered into a situation that will kill them. The sheep are dead meat.

And Jesus is saying that about . . . you. No offense. You and I are like sheep. You and I are prone to wander. We get so focused on the "green grass" of something we want that we wander away from the ways of God. Sometimes we do it by ourselves. Sometimes we flock to our friends and follow their example. Sometimes we don't want to hear what Jesus says, or we want to put our filters on him, and we drift away. We all wander. Maybe you want the green grass of success—the best grades, the starting spot, the promotion, the money that comes with extra shifts—so you wander away from the very basic things of God: real time to pray, the habit of gathering for worship every week, talking to your own family about Jesus. Maybe all your friends live in houses with two garages (or three), three bathrooms (or four), four flat-screen TVs (or five) while giving nothing to those in need, and you follow that example. You live in one of the most prosperous cultures in human history but think you don't have enough to help the poor. You and I wander.

Maybe you follow those alphas online or at school who told you to be "true to yourself" and "live authentically," and you never really stop to think if that is okay with Jesus.

You wander. Maybe you imitate the attitude of those angry commentators who think that if you're right, you don't have to be nice. Love doesn't matter that much to God, does it? You wander. **"We all, like sheep, have gone astray, each of us has turned to his own way"** (Isaiah 53:6).

And because we wander, we are in grave danger. I wish I was some creatine-filled beast of a sheep that could outrun a wolf, but I'm not. I wish that you were the one person who could sin and save themselves from danger, but you can't. Jesus called you a sheep. That means when you wander from God, when you stray, when you sin, you can't save yourself. The wolf wins every time. You and I are sheep. No offense.

But thank God! Thank God that Jesus calls himself the Good Shepherd:

> **"I am the good shepherd. The good shepherd lays down his life for the sheep. The hired hand is not the shepherd and does not own the sheep. So when he sees the wolf coming, he abandons the sheep and runs away. Then the wolf attacks the flock and scatters it. The man runs away because he is a hired hand and cares nothing for the sheep.**
>
> **"I am the good shepherd."** (John 10:11-14)

Jesus is the "Good" Shepherd. There are two or three main Greek words for "good." This one means something that is beautiful because it is of the highest moral quality.

Take all the shepherds and line them up from worst to best, and Jesus stands at the front of the line. He is beautiful because he is the best at being a shepherd.

Because unlike a "hired hand" who runs when the wolf shows up, Jesus stays. Jesus stands up for his sheep, even if we've strayed, even if he has to suffer. Which is exactly what Jesus did.

Have you ever been to Israel? Just east of Jerusalem, there's barren wilderness that plunges down to the Dead Sea. I was just there a few years ago, and it's shocking how fast you go from big city to nearly nothing. It's a dry land with hills and caves and plenty of places to run and hide. But Jesus didn't run. On the Thursday night when he was arrested and condemned to death, Jesus was on the east side of Jerusalem, praying in a garden. He knew what was about to happen. He knew his friend was betraying him and the soldiers were on the way to crucify him. He knew about the crown of thorns, the hammer and nails, the torture of the cross.

But Jesus didn't run. Why not? "I am the good shepherd. The good shepherd lays down his life for the sheep." Thank God.

Who are we? Sheep. Wandering, weak, dead-meat sheep. But whom did Jesus lay down his life for? For the sheep. For us. For me. For you. Jesus, God in human flesh, made himself dead meat. He laid down his life. He sacrificed himself so you could live. He died for your sins.

Why would Jesus do that? Think about the metaphor again. Why does a shepherd have sheep? To get something from them. Yeah, the work of a shepherd is hard, and the nights are long, but the sheep give the shepherd something—wool, clothes, food, drink, daily bread. The ROI is positive. That's why shepherds raise sheep. But not Jesus. What did Jesus need from us? He's God! He was doing pretty good before he came down from heaven. What could you and I give Jesus that he didn't already have in heaven? Nothing. So why would he come down from heaven and become our Good Shepherd? Why would he lay down his life to keep you spiritually alive? There is only one answer—love.

Jesus loves you. Jesus, who needed nothing. Jesus, whom you wandered far from—that Jesus loves you. That's why he's not just a shepherd. He's our Good Shepherd.

So what do you think about Jesus? Some people think he's crazy. "You're saying that doing what I want is wandering? Nah. You're saying I'm in danger of going to hell? No, I am fine. This is crazy."

Other people think Jesus is good. "I have wandered. I have forgotten the ways of God. I can't go back and fix it. But I have a Shepherd who saved me, a Good Shepherd who made me good with God."

So what do you say? You wouldn't be the first to be offended enough to give up on Jesus, the Bible, the Christian church. But I urge you to stay, to follow, to trust that if Jesus laid down his life for you—and he did!—then he must be good. All of us will follow someone or something in this life, and there's no one who is good like our Good Shepherd. Believe in him, and you will be safe.

STUDY QUESTIONS

1. Spend a few minutes soaking in Psalm 23, one of the most famous passages about God being our Shepherd. Note the emotions that David felt when he remembered that the Lord was shepherding his soul.

2. Read Ezekiel 34:1–16 (if time allows, read the entire chapter). Describe the problem that God's Old Testament "flock" faced. What parallels do you see with the church of Jesus' day (Pharisees, teachers of the law, the temple, etc.)?

3. Agree/Disagree: True love always requires personal sacrifice.

4. First Peter 5:1–4 connects the sheep/shepherd metaphor to Christian congregations. Pick two phrases from these verses that seem essential for a healthy church experience.

5. Jesus needed nothing from his flock yet sacrificed everything for his flock. Can you think of any human relationship that comes close to this statement? Parent/child? Employer/employee? Husband/wife?

I AM THE GATE;
WHOEVER ENTERS
THROUGH ME WILL
BE SAVED. THEY WILL
COME IN AND GO OUT,
AND FIND PASTURE.

JOHN 10:9

ONLY JESUS' VOICE SHOWS THE WAY

The Gate

Should Christians be tolerant people?

That simple question depends on how you define the word *tolerant*. If you mean the classic definition of the word, namely, to love someone who isn't believing or behaving rightly, then the answer is clear across the pages of Scripture. Christians are called to love others, even their enemies; to serve others, even those who aren't serving our Savior; and to win unbelievers over with the selflessness we learned from Jesus (1 Peter 3:1).

But if *tolerant* is defined in a more modern way, namely, to endorse and applaud distinct beliefs and behaviors, then Jesus has some harder, unfiltered words for our world.

Listen to how Jesus spoke to a group of incredibly devout

religious men who didn't accept his claims to be the Messiah: **"Very truly I tell you Pharisees, anyone who does not enter the sheep pen by the gate, but climbs in by some other way, is a thief and a robber"** (John 10:1). To teach us about tolerance, Jesus takes us to the sheep pen. Ancient sheep pens were simply open-air holding stalls for the flocks. Four walls made of sticks or stones with a small entrance in the front. That meant there was only one way in and one way out—the gate. Now technically, there were other ways you could get into the sheep pen. You could jump the fence, but why would you if you were the shepherd? The only people who snuck in were those who were up to no good. Like back when you snuck out your bedroom window to meet you-know-who at the park. You didn't walk past your parents and use the front door, because you were up to no good! But not the shepherd.

> **"The one who enters by the gate is the shepherd of the sheep. The gatekeeper opens the gate for him, and the sheep listen to his voice. He calls his own sheep by name and leads them out. When he has brought out all his own, he goes on ahead of them, and his sheep follow him because they know his voice. But they will never follow a stranger; in fact, they will run away from him because they do not recognize a stranger's voice."** (John 10:2-5)

The shepherd went through the gate and called his flock

with his familiar voice. Some pens were so big that multiple shepherds left their flocks there. But when one shepherd called, only his sheep would trot through the gate. Sheep couldn't ace the ACT, but they were smart enough to remember the voice of the one who had fed them, cared for them, loved them, protected them, saved them, and knew them by name.

Jesus paused. And the Pharisees said, "Huh? Gates and thieves and shepherds and sheep? I thought we were talking about religion?" **"Jesus used this figure of speech, but the Pharisees did not understand what he was telling them"** (John 10:6). So Jesus connected the dots and drew an incredibly intolerant picture.

"Therefore Jesus said again, 'Very truly I tell you, I am the gate for the sheep'" (verse 7).

The Pharisees said, "Wait. *The* gate?! Is Jesus saying he is the one and only legitimate way to God's flock? What does that mean about us?"

"All who have come before me are thieves and robbers, but the sheep have not listened to them" (verse 8).

"Wait. *Thieves and robbers?!* Is Jesus saying because we don't believe in him we aren't shepherds but thieves?"

"I am the gate; whoever enters through me will be saved. They will come in and go out, and find pasture" (verse 9).

"Wait. *Through me?!* Is Jesus saying the only way to be saved is through him? Is he claiming the only way to find pasture, food for your soul, is by coming through him?

What does that mean about our religion?"

"The thief comes only to steal and kill and destroy; I have come that they may have life, and have it to the full" (verse 10).

"Wait. *Kill and destroy?!* Is Jesus saying our teaching kills and his gives life? That can't be what he's saying!"

But that was exactly what Jesus was saying. He told the Pharisees again and again that God was absolutely, unequivocally, terribly intolerant of any religion that did not agree with Jesus. Old J.C. was not very PC. And his audience knew it. As soon as Jesus stopped talking, **"The Jews who heard these words . . . said, 'He is demon-possessed and raving mad'"** (verses 19,20). They couldn't tolerate a teacher who was so intolerant.

For those of us who swim in the cultural currents of modern America, it's hard to think of Jesus as so narrow-minded. But, love him or hate him, you can't honestly hear his voice and believe that he stood for anything else. Here's just a taste of what else unfiltered, intolerant Jesus said to the Pharisees: **"You do not have the love of God in your hearts"** (John 5:42). **"You will die in your sin"** (John 8:21). **"You do not belong to God"** (John 8:47). "**You belong to your father, the devil"** (John 8:44). Ouch!

But do you know the worst one? **"For God so loved the world that he gave his one and only Son, that whoever believes in him shall not perish but have eternal life. . . . But whoever does not believe stands condemned already"** (John 3:16,18). Jesus could coexist with other religions on earth, but he was absolutely clear that without him they would not coexist with God in heaven. "The road to God is narrow," he sighed, "and only few will find it."

Jesus was in no way suggesting a lack of love for non-Christians. Christ loves the world, and Christians should too. Christians should be the best neighbors their non-Christian neighbors have ever had. We should shovel Muslim driveways, laugh with Jewish children, have Hindus over for dinner, defend doubters' reputations, bring meals for Buddhists with newborn babies, and bring tissues to witches whose loved ones die. But when it comes to God, Christians are to be radically intolerant of other beliefs. Just like Jesus.

What a warm and fuzzy teaching, right? Jesus' words are a bitter pill for the people pleasers and thin-skinned among us. You might break out in an anxious sweat over the idea of saying to a Muslim, Mormon, or moral friend, "You need Jesus. There is no other way, no other gate, no other voice that can save you." No, that's not easy. Maybe that's why some surveys reveal that the majority of young, self-professing Christians say, "Jesus is just one of many ways to God." They insist Jesus is much more tolerant than Jesus himself claimed.

But could it be true that intolerance and love aren't mutually exclusive? Is it possible that being incredibly compassionate and staunchly unaccepting actually go hand in hand? It is not only possible but completely logical. Think of a mom who checks the nutritional facts before feeding her sons or checks the text messages between her teenage daughters and her new friends. She won't endorse and applaud everything she sees, right? She can't accept something she believes isn't good for the ones she loves most.

Is it at all possible that some teachings, some beliefs, some opinions, some teachers are so dangerous for our souls that a loving Father won't tolerate them either? Could it be true that Jesus is so exclusive, so intolerant, because he loves you? Yes! Jesus doesn't budge on his beliefs because he loves you. Here's why—please don't miss this next line—*because every religion besides Jesus tells you that you have to save you.*

In Christian-ese, we call that *work righteousness*, the idea that if you work hard enough, you can be right with God. You can be righteous. But that idea simply won't work. Because what's right to God is doing right all the time. What's right is never lying to your parents, even if you know they'll be mad. What's right is listening to people you don't agree with without interrupting. What's right is being grateful for what God has given instead of complaining about what he hasn't. What's right is praying for your annoying coworkers, not venting about them. What's right is agreeing with Jesus even if people label you, not keeping your faith to yourself just so they don't. Yet every religion—every one!—from Pharisaism to Judaism to Buddhism to Hinduism to generic moralism all tell you that you can save you. You can work hard enough to be righteous. Jesus knows you can't. So he won't smile and wave as you walk down that road. He will wave his intolerant hands and shout his unfiltered, offensive message: "This will destroy you!"

Instead he said, **"I am the gate; whoever enters through me will be saved. They will come in and go out, and find pasture"** (John 10:9). Through Jesus, we are saved and delivered from God's anger. From the treadmill of making it up to God. From the pressure to be good enough today to make up for the bad of yesterday. From wondering if God loves us today. Through Jesus, we find pasture. The green grass called grace. To know you and I are loved today not because of what we did but because our Good Shepherd laid down his life for us. To know we are safe from our past today not because we've built big enough walls with our works but because our gate is Jesus and nothing can get past him. Through Jesus, we have life, life to the full. We have life even though we've been bad, dropped the ball, disappointed others, disappointed ourselves. Through Jesus, the work is done, and those who believe are already right with God! Because Jesus wouldn't tolerate losing you or me, he laid down his life.

That's the voice of Jesus. We listen to it. You might say I'm a Christian because I was raised that way. Perhaps true, but I've learned enough to know this—no one else's God will take me. If I believed the Koran, I would have to stack all my sins on a scale and pray Allah would forget about most of them. If I believed the Book of Mormon, I would have to hope the heavenly Father would look past my "good works" done with an inward desire to be praised. If I were a moralistic American, I would beg that the stories and pictures of my past would never go viral. I don't listen to those voices. Because I hear a voice that sounds so much sweeter. It knows my name. It says, "Mike, it is finished. I love you. You are mine. I am the gate. Through me everything is good with God." I, we, won't tolerate any voice less beautiful than that.

STUDY QUESTIONS

1. Doors keep dangerous weather/animals/people outside. Connect this basic definition to Jesus, who is called the door/the gate.

2. "He calls his own sheep by name" (John 10:3). What is so powerful about the words *calls*, *his own*, and *by name*?

3. Jesus calls non-Jesus-based religious leaders "thieves" and "robbers" (John 10:8). What do works-based religions (i.e., if you do enough good, you will be right with God) steal from people?

4. John 10:10 has become a rather famous verse in modern times. Why do you suppose that is? And what exactly does "life to the full" mean?

5. While there is plenty of confrontation in John 10:1–10, there is also endless comfort. Which verse personally brings you the most comfort out of Jesus' tough and tender message?

I AM THE VINE; YOU
ARE THE BRANCHES.
IF YOU REMAIN IN ME
AND I IN YOU, YOU
WILL BEAR MUCH
FRUIT; APART FROM ME
YOU CAN DO NOTHING.

JOHN 15:5

CONNECTED TO JESUS, YOU WILL GROW

The Vine

There are three crucial moments in every Christian's spiritual journey. Sooner or later, if you follow the real, unfiltered Jesus, you'll face these incredible challenging moments that will test your commitment to Christ.

The first crucial moment is *confusion*. It is incredibly confusing as a Christian when you're trying to be good, but your life is really bad. You're trying to follow Jesus, trying to do what the Bible says, but instead of getting better, your life gets worse. You start going to church, but then you lose your job. You get baptized, but then the bills start stacking up. You pray every day, but your body is still falling apart. And that's confusing. Why wouldn't God help you? Why wouldn't God say yes to your prayer when you're in so much pain? No one is perfect, but why would God let bad things happen to God-fearing people? It's confusing.

The second crucial moment is *condemnation*. Condemnation is when you feel bad because you've been bad. You spent all weekend worrying and grumbling and freaking out, totally forgetting about God and his power and his promises. Which is what you've pretty much been doing your whole life. Or you got into it again—arguing, raising your voice, trying to be right. And after your emotions cool down, you realize how ungodly it all was. Or maybe you look back on something in your past—pushing for her abortion, being unfaithful to your partner—and you feel . . . dirty, unworthy. Christians are supposed to be free from shame, but you don't feel that way. That's condemnation.

The third crucial moment is *temptation*. Temptation is when you're seriously second-guessing if you want to stick with Jesus. You get what God is supposedly saying in the Bible, but do you really want to remain a Bible-believing, Jesus-following kind of person? You know people who aren't repenting of their sins, aren't trying to obey the Bible, aren't trusting in Jesus, and they seem fine. In fact, some of them are pretty happy. So do you really want to stick around? That's temptation.

Confusion, condemnation, temptation. Why is life so bad? Why am I so bad? Is Christianity really that good? Those three moments happen every day in churches and to Christian people. Ever been there? Are you there right now? You might be one accident away from confusion, one sin away from condemnation, and one friend away from temptation. You're going to face these crucial moments too.

Jesus knows that. That's why Jesus, the night before he died on a cross, gave us a powerful metaphor about himself that helps all of us deal with the confusion, condemnation, and temptation. It's what we find in John chapter 15.

Let's start with confusion. If you've ever questioned God because of your pain, listen to what Jesus said in verses 1 and 2: **"I am the true vine, and my Father is the gardener. He cuts off every branch in me that bears no fruit, while every branch that does bear fruit he prunes so that it will be even more fruitful."** Jesus takes us out to the garden, to the place where vines and branches push out grapes to produce good wine. Notice what Jesus says about good branches, the ones that bear fruit. He (God) prunes them so they will be even more fruitful. He prunes. He cuts. He snips and leaves his best branches wounded.

Imagine for a second that you are a vine and I am a gardener. If I pulled out shears, as a vine you'd scream—"No! You monster! You murderer!" But you'd be wrong, because the reason you prune a good branch is so it becomes "even more fruitful." By pruning, I can focus a plant's limited resources to producing fruit instead of growing a bunch of new shoots. If fruit is the goal, then pruning is not confusing.

That's what Marty told me. Marty and his family own a vineyard in central Wisconsin, so I emailed him these words from Jesus. He told me about the process of pruning and then added these words: "The biggest mistake people make is not pruning aggressively. The better the pruning, the more fruitful the grapes will be."

That is essential when suffering is leaving you confused. If God's goal for you is the "fruit" of faith and love and focus on things above, pruning makes total sense. Sometimes if all you have is success in school and sports and life, you end up really arrogant. But failure prunes you and makes you humble like Jesus. Sometimes if you've never suffered, it's hard to feel compassion or sympathy for people in pain. But suffering prunes you and makes you a bit more like Jesus. Sometimes it takes a lot of mess to end up with a ministry. You have to go through it before you have something wise to say about it. So even if you can't see it, don't be confused by it. God might be pruning you aggressively, taking away a blessing you really loved—your health, your dreams, your plans for the future. It doesn't mean he's punishing you. He's pruning you. He's preparing you. In all things God is working for the good. Believe that, and you won't be confused.

You'll be more fruitful than ever before.

That's confusion, but what about condemnation? What if you do believe in Jesus, but you haven't been all that fruitful? How do you know that God isn't going to cut you off and throw you into the fire? Jesus continues, **"You are already clean because of the word I have spoken to you"** (verse 3). Ah, I love this! Jesus is saying something shocking: "You guys are already clean." When God looks at you, he sees a soul that is clean, a soul that is good, a soul that is good enough for heaven. He's not waiting until you get better or make those big changes or kick all your bad habits or improve your spiritual résumé. No, you are already clean.

How could Jesus say that? This was the night before he died, and he was talking to guys who were hours away from denying and abandoning him. Their faith was so flawed. How could they be "already clean"? Jesus said, "Because of the word I have spoken to you." The word of Jesus, his message of forgiveness and salvation, had the power to make them clean. When God looks at a Christian, because of the blood of Christ, he declares with authority—"Already clean!" And if you believe in Jesus, this is what God is declaring over you. You feel dirty, but God says, "Already clean."

Let's apply that. But what if you have a record, have done time, are on parole? "Already clean." But what if you're still struggling with the same sins you did a year ago? "Already clean." But what if you were a rebellious kid? "Already clean." But what if you messed up your marriage? "Already clean." But what if you said . . . "Already clean." Yes! "You are already clean because of the word I have spoken to you." Do you regret your sins? Me too. Do you wish you could go back and redo life? Me too. But Jesus shed his blood to make sure that there is no condemnation, that you, right now, are already clean because of the word of his grace.

Which is a clue to how to handle our last critical moment—temptation. Why remain with Jesus? Here's Jesus' answer:

> **"Remain in me, as I also remain in you. No branch can bear fruit by itself; it must remain in the vine.**

Neither can you bear fruit unless you remain in me.

"I am the vine; you are the branches. If you remain in me and I in you, you will bear much fruit; apart from me you can do nothing. If you do not remain in me, you are like a branch that is thrown away and withers; such branches are picked up, thrown into the fire and burned. If you remain in me and my words remain in you, ask whatever you wish, and it will be done for you. This is to my Father's glory, that you bear much fruit, showing yourselves to be my disciples.

"As the Father has loved me, so have I loved you. Now remain in my love." (verses 4-9)

Remain, remain, remain, remain, remain, remain, remain, remain, remain. Nine times Jesus teaches, urges, and pleads that you would remain with him.

Why? Consider the tale of Stan the Branch. Once upon a time, Stan was stuck in his usual spot on the trunk of a thick oak tree. The trunk was strong, and Stan's leaves were beautiful in the fall. But sometimes as he looked down on the world, he wondered what it would be like to be a squirrel, to go wherever and do whatever he wanted, not to be stuck to the trunk. That's why one day when a fierce wind whipped through the park, Stan leaned into it until—snap!—he was free! He dropped into a soft bed of green grass and laughed as the wind rolled him to places he had never been before. That night Stan fell asleep in his plush bed with stars twinkling overhead. But in the morning when Stan woke up, he felt dry. Thirsty. Weak. Days passed, and the thirst got worse. His back tightened up, and his fingers turned brittle. Until one day a man walked up to Stan and saw not a branch but a dried-up, leafless stick that would soon be tossed into a fire and burned.

"Remain in me," Jesus says to your soul. "Without me, you are like a body without bread—dead. Without me you are like a sheep without a shepherd—dead. Without me, you are like a branch without a vine—dead. Stick with me, or you will be a stick, dried out, lacking life with God." Branches are not independent beings. They die in their independence. We do too.

Do you see why I'm saying this? Because Jesus said this. I know that some churches are all about the fire and brimstone, that they often underemphasize the love of God, but we must not underemphasize the holiness of God. We must not put out the fire and act as if hell doesn't exist, because it was Jesus who said it. And he said that without remaining in him, hell is where souls will end up.

You can refuse to repent. You can do what you want, believe what you want, and behave how you want. You can walk away from Jesus, do what you want with your body, hold on to your money, and come up with your own journey. You don't have to stick with Jesus. But Jesus wants you to know that then you'll become a stick. You'll have no connection to his cross, his forgiveness, or his salvation. You'll still have to stand before God and be judged, but now there will be no one to save you. No one to erase your wrongs. No one to make you clean in God's eyes. No one to make you good enough for a better place.

So remain, remain, remain, remain, remain, remain, remain, remain, remain in Jesus! Don't be a stick. Stay stuck to Jesus. And if that sounds like a threat (it is, in part), then don't forget Jesus' final words: **"As the Father has loved me, so have I loved you. Now remain in my love"** (verse 9). Let that verse blow your mind. "As the Father has loved me (Jesus)—that perfect, flawless, constant, eternal, glorious love—so have I loved you." What?! Jesus loves you that much. So much that he forgives you and sticks with you, he has compassion on you and cleanses you, he makes you happy because he cares about you, and he prunes you because he wants what is best for you. No one has ever loved you like Jesus. Not your dog. Not your grandma. No one will have time for you like Jesus. No one will be there for you like Jesus. No one will welcome you into heaven like Jesus. So remain in his love. When you are tempted to think there's something better out there, remember that the love you get from Jesus is as good as it gets.

And that is how you get through it. Confused by your pain? God is pruning you for something better. Condemned by your sin? You are already clean because of Jesus. Tempted to bail on the Bible? There is no love out there like the love of Jesus.

Max Lucado knows that. When the now famous Christian author was 16, he got drunk, which was a big deal because Max came from a family of drunks. His father had warned him of the alcoholism that ran in their family and the misery it brought with it. But despite the warning, Max got drunk. And then he did it again. And again. And a hundred more times through his teenage years. The guilt he felt was heavier than a steel chain. But then Jesus set him free. Max could take you to the city, to the church, to the very seat where he heard a pastor preach about the forgiveness of Jesus, how God's grace is greater than our sin, how the cross conquers our condemnation. Max believed it. Max believed in him. That's how he literally, spiritually, eternally got clean.

Friend, today or tomorrow, you'll face confusion or condemnation or temptation. But remain in Jesus, and you'll more than get through it.

STUDY QUESTIONS

1. Read the rest of Jesus' sermon in John 15:9-17. What ideas from verses 1-8 is Jesus repeating/reinforcing? What new ideas does he add in these verses?

2. Christians who know their Bible should not be shocked, jarred, or confused by suffering. If you feel that way today, read James 1:2–8; Romans 5:1–5; and/or 1 Peter 4:12–16.

3. Looking back on your life, can you identify a time of "pruning," when God cut back on your blessings in order to give you something better in the future?

4. There are billions of people who do not "remain" in Jesus yet do kind things for their fellow man. How do you reconcile that fact with Jesus' claim in John 15:5?

5. "You are already clean" (John 15:3). If you are studying these words alone, find a mirror and repeat this stunning statement of grace to yourself. If you are in a group, look someone in the eye with gospel seriousness and share this beautiful news.

I AM THE WAY
AND THE TRUTH AND
THE LIFE. NO ONE
COMES TO THE FATHER
EXCEPT THROUGH ME.

JOHN 14:6

JESUS IS THE ONLY WAY TO HEAVEN

The Way, the Truth, and the Life

Every time I stand up in front of my congregation, I am essentially trying to do the same thing: study the Bible, study my congregation, and unite the two. Study the Bible means what God said, what Jesus did, and what God is like. Then I relate it to people's lives in the most personal, powerful, emotional way that I can. And when I want to do that—connect with people, make them feel like I had cameras in their homes (but not in a creepy way)—I have a simple thing that I almost always do. I think about the five *F*s. I imagine what might be troubling them when it comes to the five areas of life that all of us care about dearly.

Here are the five *F*s. Maybe you've got some *family* problems. You want to be close to your family, but your mom is just the way she is and your dad is distant and your siblings have never been that tight. Or you want to start a family, but dating is messy. Online dating is overwhelming. Guys are weird, and women are . . . I'll let you finish that sentence. Your grandpa died. Your son is making dumb decisions, turning his back on Jesus. Do I have your attention?

Others of us have *friend* problems. No one can be all that happy without good friends, but finding them when you're 6 or 16 or 46 is not that easy. And finding time for friends isn't either. And finding new friends when your old friends are the reason you ended up where you did isn't either.

Then there are your *fitness*/physical problems—surgery, recovery, disability, lungs, liver, cancer, Alzheimer's, intubation, and infection.

Then some have no financial peace but tons of *financial* problems—you can't pay for college, can't keep up with car payments, can't keep everyone on the payroll. You check the numbers every day, and every night you feel the same pressure.

And even if you and I are people of faith, we have *faith* problems, don't we? We feel like we're behind, that everyone else's faith is better. We get stuck in some bad habit or relapse into old temptations. We make big promises to change things, but we don't change.

Family, friends, fitness, finances, faith—the five *F*s. Do you have issues with any of that?

If that's you, what do you do? When one or more of those things is troubling you, what do you do? I know you do something. You sit there and think about it while fear and anxiety dominate your brain. You run away to a bar, a pill, a device so you don't have to think about how bad it is. You work like crazy to fix it and carry the pressure of making everything better. We all do something. What do you do?

Jesus knows what we should do. The night before he died, he was hanging out with his closest friends in Jerusalem when he dropped some troubling news on them: "One of you will betray me. Even you, Peter, will deny me." The disciples were stunned. Their thoughts started swirling. The anxiety shallowed their breath, and they looked at each other in panic. And that's when Jesus told them exactly what to do, the exact same thing he would say to you.

"Do not let your hearts be troubled. You believe in God; believe also in me" (John 14:1). At first, the unfiltered Jesus doesn't seem very helpful—"Don't! You're worried? Well, stop it!" But then he shows them how—"You believe in God. You aren't atheists. You all believe that God exists, that God cares, that God controls all things. You aren't unbelievers who have to sit around and hope it gets better. No, you believe in God; believe also in me."

The phrase Jesus uses here in the original Greek of the Bible is interesting. The word *in* from "believe in" has this idea of direction, like you're looking toward or at something. Picture it like this. Jesus is saying, "You are people of faith, people who believe in God. So turn *toward* me. Look *at* me. Put your attention in my *direction*."

Why? Because there are really incredible benefits to

believing in God during moments like that. Jesus explains why being a believer is such a blessing: **"My Father's house has many rooms; if that were not so, would I have told you that I am going there to prepare a place for you? And if I go and prepare a place for you, I will come back and take you to be with me that you also may be where I am"** (John 14:2,3). When life is hard, don't forget about heaven! Jesus calls heaven "my Father's house," that perfect place where no one is lonely, sad, angry, or worried, where you feel good and then feel better and then even better than before. In heaven no one fights or loses touch, no one winces in pain or wonders if they'll have enough to get by. No, people party in heaven. There is so much love it makes falling in love look lame. Wedding vows and holding grandbabies down here seems lame compared to life up there.

Why? Because God is there! It's called his "Father's house" because that's where he lives. That's where God is. Jesus isn't worried about golf or pets or marriage vows, because God is there. You get to be in the same room where God is! You might flip out if Luke Bryan or Beyoncé or Giannis Antetokounmpo was in the same room as you. Imagine being in the place where God is!

And believe this: "In my Father's house are many rooms." Heaven is not like getting tickets for a sold-out show or a hotel room on game-day weekend. There's room, Jesus says, for you. This is a stunning statement of love, because Jesus, seconds earlier, had said, "Peter, you will deny me. You won't slip up just once. You'll say you don't even know me three times in a row." But then Jesus continues, "For you. I'm preparing a place in heaven for you. For you too, Peter."

And for you too. You might think you're not good enough to get to heaven. You're not worthy to be where God is. And—you know what?—you're right. You're not. Because you are just like Peter, just like me. You mess up. You sin. You don't deserve it. But Jesus still gives it. He promises, "I am going to prepare a place for you. I am going to finish the job, die on a cross, rise from the grave, return to my Father. I'll do the work. I'll make you good." Notice the subject of Jesus' verbs, the person doing the work. It's Jesus. And if Jesus does everything, if he lives and dies and rises and forgives and saves and redeems, then people like Peter and me and you can "afford" a room. Through believing in Jesus, even people like us can be with a God like that!

So here's Jesus' quick tip: When your heart is troubled, don't act like an atheist. Don't think that this is all there is. Believe in God.

Turn toward God. Remember that you are one day closer to your room. Tell your heart that your story has a perfect ending. Preach the promises of Jesus: "He's coming back for me so I may be where he is."

It makes me think of the pastor who was suddenly told he only had six weeks to live. After the doctor broke the news, the pastor got stuck. Everything he tried to think ended with the same words—*six weeks to live*. But then one day he turned "toward" the gospel of John and believed what Jesus said. He read this promise: **"I give** [my sheep] **eternal life, and . . . no one can snatch them out of my hand"** (John 10:28). Eternal life. The pastor reasoned, "If Jesus said 'eternal life,' why am I thinking about six weeks?"

If you believe in Jesus, you know how to get your hands on eternal life. Look at these last verses:

> **"You know the way to the place where I am going."**
>
> **Thomas said to him, "Lord, we don't know where you are going, so how can we know the way?"**
>
> **Jesus answered, "I am the way and the truth and the life. No one comes to the Father except through me."** (John 14:4-6)

I love Thomas. He didn't get it, so he decided to admit it. "Jesus, how can we know the way when we don't know the where? How can we figure out the directions if we don't know the destination?"

The other day I told Siri, "Give me the directions," and Siri replied (can you guess?), "Where are you going?" That's what Thomas said too, so Jesus told him in the simplest terms: "I am the way to the Father. My Father's house is the destination, and I am the way to get there. Even guys like you, fishermen and tax collectors and very-apparent sinners, can get to the perfection of heaven, that is, if you come through me."

Jesus' words here are classic, perhaps one of the top ten most famous Bible passages. But they are both offensive and awesome at the same time. Do you see why? The offensive part makes me think of Robin from the bus. I was in Chicago with a pastor friend, taking a bus at the airport, when a really friendly extrovert named Robin did what extroverts do and started a conversation. She quickly learned that we were both pastors and then, just as quickly, shared how she thought that all religions and faiths were ways to get to God. My friend gently pushed back on her belief with Jesus' words: "I am the way." But Robin replied, "Well, all three of us know that in the original Greek, Jesus did not say 'the way.' He said, 'a way.'" I hadn't memorized any Greek Bible passages, so I had to check. Was Robin right? Was Jesus cool with many roads to God? Have some of his followers twisted his words and become overly exclusive?

Well, no offense to Robin, but Robin was wrong. She had put a filter on Jesus. Check it out. Here are the Greek words from Jesus: *Ἐγώ εἰμι ἡ ὁδὸς καὶ ἡ ἀλήθεια καὶ ἡ ζωή*. And here is the literal English translation: "I am the way and the truth and the life." It's not complicated grammar. And there repeated before *way* and *truth* and *life* is a little Greek letter that looks like a fancy *n*. It means "the." Jesus said, "I am *the* way." That's why no one can get to God except through him.

I can understand why Robin wouldn't want to believe that. The unfiltered Jesus was denying the claim that there are many paths up the mountain that we call God. He was saying, as simply as he could, that there is only one key that opens the door to the Father's house, only one route that connects earth to heaven, only one password that gives us access to above, only one way for us to get to God. That's through Jesus.

Heaven is perfect, and only perfect people are allowed. If you've sinned, and you have, you are not perfect. You could do your best for the rest of your life, but you still wouldn't be perfect. That's why we all need Jesus. Only he can make us perfect. Only he can cleanse us from sins and make us good enough to be with God. And he has. He left the room that night and went to his cross for you. He wanted you to have a way, to know the way, to escape this broken world. And if you believe in Jesus, you do know the way. You are on the way to seeing God!

So let's get back to the question: What do you do when something goes wrong with your family or friends or fitness or finances or faith? I like this answer—GOD ASAP. Turn toward God as fast as possible. Think about your eternal future, your room in your Father's house, the life you have because Jesus is the way. Grab your Bible, and open to John chapter 14 or Romans chapter 8. Google "Bible passages about heaven," and turn your eyes toward your for-sure future. Of course we pray for healing right now. Of course we work to improve what we can right here. But no matter what happens with him or her or you, you have forever with God. You have eternal life in Jesus' name.

You believe in God, right? Then believe in Jesus.

My friend did. My friend was facing a serious legal

situation that was out of his control. A judge would decide if he would be free to change out of his orange jumpsuit and join us for worship or if he would spend decades in prison. He was afraid. I was too. I thought he should be set free, but that wasn't my call, and I didn't have the whole story. Just before the verdict, my friend wrote me a letter, updating me on the case. Right on the bottom he wrote three words that put a smile on my face, words that proved that he wasn't just sitting and waiting; he was turning and believing. He wrote, "God's got this." Yes, he does. All the time.

In this world, you will have trouble. But you believe in God. Turn toward him today, and you will find peace.

STUDY QUESTIONS

1. What does it look like when a follower of Jesus is "troubled"? What do they think/feel/do in such moments?

2. Name one trouble you have faced/are facing for each of the five *F*s—family, friends, fitness, finances, faith. After each one, read John 14:1 aloud.

3. The Greek of John 14:1 can be rightly translated a few ways. Comment on the meaning of each of them:
   a. "You believe in God. Believe also in me."
   b. "You believe in God. You believe also in me."
   c. "Believe in God. Believe also in me."

4. Evaluate: Remembering that this life is *so* short and your life in heaven is *so* long is essential to calming your troubled heart. (Read 2 Corinthians 4:16–18 for Paul's answer.)

5. This chapter urged you to run to GOD ASAP. Come up with a specific plan that you can follow when your heart is troubled. (For example: When I feel troubled, I will read Psalm 23.)

I AM THE RESURRECTION
AND THE LIFE. THE
ONE WHO BELIEVES IN
ME WILL LIVE, EVEN
THOUGH THEY DIE;
AND WHOEVER LIVES
BY BELIEVING IN ME
WILL NEVER DIE.

JOHN 11:25,26

JESUS MEANS LIFE AFTER DEATH FOR YOU

The Resurrection and the Life

In this final chapter, we're going to take on one more claim that Jesus made. And it's the reason why Easter is a big deal. It's not just an average Sunday, and I bet you knew that. Easter baskets, Easter bunnies, Easter eggs, and—most important—Easter brunch. What other major American holiday puts its focus on breakfast? Only Easter. If you love scrambled eggs and cinnamon roll sugar highs, you know Easter is a big deal. And you feel it at church too, right? Easter dresses, Easter dress shirts, Easter flowers, and—most important—Easter donuts. Even if you're not an every-Sunday kind of church person, you might show up at Easter, because Easter really is a big deal.

But I would suggest that Easter is a big deal not because

of the brunch or the baskets but because it helps you answer two of life's biggest questions: What about Jesus, and what about death? What do you personally do with Jesus, and what do you do with death?

First, what do you do with Jesus? What do you believe about him? As you've read throughout this book, the real Jesus, the unfiltered and unedited Jesus, made some massive claims about himself, statements that really won't let you be "kind of" Christian. Jesus divided people when he claimed to be the Bread from heaven, the food your soul needs to survive or it will die, and the Light of the world, without whom you are spiritually in the dark. He claimed to be the Good Shepherd that a wandering, weak sheep like you needs so you don't die eternally. Jesus doubled down and dared to say that he was the only way to heaven, the only truth on earth, the only life that could lead you to God. What do you think about that? Do you believe it? Do you believe him? If so, he would have to become the most important part of your life, so do you believe that? Easter can help you answer that question.

Next, what about you and death? Sorry to mess with your sugar high, but you are going to die. My daughter didn't want me to say that part when I presented it to her one Easter Sunday. I tried to give her an early preview of my sermon, but my youngest wasn't a fan. "Maya," I said, "I think I'm going to start the Easter sermon with, 'You're all gonna die.'"

But she pushed back, "Dad, it's Easter. It's supposed to be happy."

"But how can I talk about the resurrection of the dead unless I talk about death," I explained.

"Dad," she repeated, "it's Easter."

She was probably right, but, for real, you're going to die.

From small losses to your big ending, death is something we all have in common. I know we'd rather not think about that, but, seriously, what do you do with that? How do you cope with that? How do you have hope in that? I bet you know someone who passed away in the last year or someone who faced death like never before. God doesn't want you not to have an answer to that unavoidable question, and Easter can help you answer it.

So let's talk about brunch and bunnies some other time. Here I want to explain why Easter is the way to answer the biggest questions about you and Jesus and you and death. That's what makes Easter a big deal.

First, let's talk about you and Jesus. Easter is a big deal because *Jesus stopped being dead.* Do you know the history? About two thousand years ago, on a fateful Thursday night, Jesus, the man who claimed to be God, was betrayed by one of his best friends. Sold out for a sack of silver, Jesus was arrested, tried, and condemned to die on a cross just outside the walls of ancient Jerusalem.

And he really died. In 2017, 60 miles north of London, archaeologists discovered the ancient remains of a man who had been crucified by the Romans, proven by the two-inch iron nail smashed through his right heel bone. It was similar to another victim whose heel bone is displayed in Jerusalem.

Scientists detected signs of trauma on the decomposed body, but the most disturbing detail was the indentation next to the nail hole. Apparently, the Romans tried to drive the nail through his foot, but it didn't work, so they ripped it out and tried again next door. That man died gruesomely on a cross. Just like Jesus. After six hours of torture, Jesus of Nazareth took his final breath and was pronounced dead.

But then the following Sunday, Jesus stopped being dead. Do you know the history? His female friends went to mourn his death, but the boulder that served as the front door of his grave had been rolled away. His body was gone, and word was that Jesus had stopped being dead. "He is risen!" is what the witnesses said. Don't dismiss them as gullible, because they were anything but. At first the disciples didn't believe it, Thomas doubted it, and a scholar named Saul denied it. Until they all saw it. Until they all saw Jesus. And the resurrection instantly gave them faith to follow Jesus as their Lord, Savior, and God.

Within years of the resurrection, Christians like the newly convinced Saul (now Paul) were passing along this creed, an ancient statement of faith:

> **For what I received I passed on to you as of first importance: that Christ died for our sins according to the Scriptures, that he was buried, that he was raised on the third day according to the Scriptures, and that he appeared to Cephas, and then to the Twelve. After that, he appeared to more than five**

> **hundred of the brothers and sisters at the same time, most of whom are still living, though some have fallen asleep.** (1 Corinthians 15:3-8)

Easter is a big deal because it proves that Jesus is more than a good guy or a noble example. He is the Christ, the Messiah, the Chosen One, the Lord who came down to save us from our sins. People like Paul changed their minds about Jesus because Easter gave them enough evidence to do so.

How about you? If Easter happened, then Jesus is the biggest deal of all, worthy to be your number-one passion, your every-Sunday priority, your Lord and Savior, your Light and Shepherd, your Way, your Truth, your Life. If Easter happened, if God came down from heaven to forgive sin and conquer death, then following this Jesus with your whole heart is the only sensible next step. If you're not a Christian or not a church person or someone who stops by a church once or twice a year, I want to challenge you to reconsider Jesus, who he is, what he did, and where he fits in your life.

Maybe you think it's too late, that it's been too long, that you're too (whatever) to belong with Jesus. It makes me think of my Uber driver. A year ago, I lost my voice, and my car wouldn't start on the same day. I ordered an Uber. This woman picked me up in a pimped-out Jeep. We got into a hilarious me-texting, her-talking conversation and laughed the whole way to church. But that's when Jesus came up. She mentioned how expensive gas was. I texted, "Time for that Prius!" She laughed. I added, "It's what Jesus wants."

She suddenly turned serious and said, "Well . . . it wouldn't be the first time I disappointed Jesus." Man, I wonder what she meant.

Maybe you are there today, thinking Jesus is too disappointed, that your story is too messy, that you're done after today. Don't. That Friday on the cross and that Sunday at the tomb were as much for you as they were for me. Jesus died for our sins—ours—and he was raised for us. So take a next step. Stay connected. Come back. Easter is big enough. Jesus is big enough to save you too.

Ready for part two? Easter is a big deal because of you and Jesus, and it's also a big deal because *you are going to die*. I am going to die. Sooner or later, suddenly or right when expected, you and I are going to die. How do you feel about that?

If it bothers you, I don't blame you. In the beginning, God didn't create things to die or say goodbye. Visitations and funerals and graveside services weren't what our Father intended. That's why in the Bible, death is called our enemy. That's why when Jesus himself went to a funeral, he wept. In this broken world, things die. Dreams die. Hopes die. Friendships die. Flowers wilt, bread grows stale, and divorce kills sacred vows. Widows walk into church every week. Miscarriages happen every month. A time will come when you will attend far more funerals than weddings. How will you handle the death that is everywhere in this life?

How about Easter? The same Jesus who rose on Easter morning once said, **"I am the resurrection and the life. The one who believes in me will live, even though they die;**

and whoever lives by believing in me will never die" (John 11:25,26). Jesus wasn't denying the obvious truth—even though we die. He knew even his most faithful followers get sick, get old, get cancer. Being a believer doesn't mean you won't suffer.

But in a way, you won't die. Your life won't end if you're with the One who called himself "the life." Jesus promised that whenever your last breath comes, everyone who believes in him will actually live like never before. It might be painful, but suddenly—in a blink of an eye—it will get unbelievably wonderful. The Jesus who predicted and pulled off his own resurrection will repeat the miracle for you, giving you life after death. Do you believe in Jesus? Then you will live. You will never die. Death will not have the last word.

Think what that means. It means that every single believer in Jesus gets heaven. Paradise. Where nothing fails or fades. Where no one gets sick; where nothing is lost. Do you ever think about life after death? It makes jelly beans and Jell-O squares look like nothing (and that's saying something!). It makes spring break stink and the Florida sun seem lame. In heaven, you get to see God. Nothing hurts. No one cries for help. Just Jesus and light and life.

Some people are terrified to die. Not you and me. Because Easter is a big deal—the historical, definitive proof that death doesn't win. Jesus does. Sin doesn't wear the crown. Jesus does. The grave isn't getting away with it. Nah. We have Jesus, the Son of God, the Resurrection and the Life. And every day from now until then is not one day closer to death; it's one day closer to the best life you can imagine.

Last month I took my first-ever hike through the beautiful desert of southern Arizona. Think prickly pear, towering saguaro cacti, multicolored mountains, and a Wisconsin boy escaping the snow for the southwestern sun. There was only one problem—I got lost.

Apparently, I got off the path and ended up lost in a thick mix of pokey plants and burrowed holes that looked like snakes could live in them. Oops. I climbed over boulders, ducked under branches, and tried to figure out where in the world I was. But then it hit me. There's an app for that! I had downloaded an app with a map of the trail and—what do you know? It showed me right where I was and how to get back. And once I got to the trail, it stopped being scary and started getting gorgeous.

Jesus is like that app. The unfiltered Jesus is full of grace and truth. He shows you the way to be with God, the way to face death and the way to live life.

STUDY QUESTIONS

1. Read the entire story of the death and resurrection of Lazarus (John 11:1–44), noting the actions that backed up Jesus' bold words: "I am the resurrection and the life."

2. Martha was honest with her frustrations (John 11:21) yet rooted in her faith (verse 22). As you read her interaction with Jesus, how can she be a good example as you go through struggles in your life?

3. What caused Jesus to weep in John 11:35? Name at least three causes.

4. According to John 11:40–42, what was the ultimate point of raising Lazarus from the grave? According to verse 53, what other effect did this miracle have? How do your answers fit into the bigger themes of this book and the gospel of John?

5. Ponder John 11:43,44. What exactly raised Jesus' friend from the dead? How does your answer affect the way you view reading your Bible, going to church, or sharing your faith with a skeptical friend?

CONCLUSION

Throughout this book, you've read the way Jesus described himself in his own words. The unedited, unfiltered Jesus was, without a doubt, offensive and divisive. Despite his ability to heal the sick and raise the dead, the vast majority of his original audience didn't like him due to his extreme claims of divinity (I'm God) and authority (I always get the last word).

How about you? When Jesus' words are hard to embrace personally and even harder to endorse publicly, will you remain with Jesus? John's gospel, which retells the story of some of Jesus' most offensive moments, gives us a compelling reason to follow Jesus: **"But these are written that you may believe that Jesus is the Messiah, the Son of God, and that by believing you may have life in his name"** (John 20:31).

Yes, Jesus is divisive. Yes, Jesus is offensive. But the name of Jesus is the only way to be fully forgiven, completely pure, and absolutely good enough to live with God. So no matter how many of your friends stay or go, I pray that you stick with Jesus and find eternal life in his name. **"What is more, I consider everything a loss because of the surpassing worth of knowing Christ Jesus my Lord, for whose sake I have lost all things. I consider them garbage, that I may gain Christ"** (Philippians 3:8). No matter what he costs you, Jesus is worth it.

NOTES

1. Gregory A. Smith, "About Three-in-Ten U.S. Adults Are Now Religiously Unaffiliated," Pew Research Center, December 14, 2021, https://www.pewresearch.org/religion/2021/12/14/about-three-in-ten-u-s-adults-are-now-religiously-unaffiliated/.

2. Nancy Armour, "Tony Dungy Shows His True Values With Hateful Tweet That Puts Transgender Kids at Risk," *USA Today*, updated January 20, 2023, https://www.usatoday.com/story/sports/columnist/nancy-armour/2023/01/19/tony-dungy-bigotry-vulnerable-transgender-kids-risk/11085306002/.

3. C. S. Lewis, *Mere Christianity* (New York: HarperCollins, 2001), 52.

ABOUT THE AUTHOR

Pastor Mike Novotny pours his Jesus-based joy into his ministry as a pastor at The CORE (Appleton, Wisconsin) and as the lead speaker for Time of Grace, a global media ministry that connects people to God through television, print, and digital resources. He is unafraid to bring grace and truth to the toughest topics of our time and has taken on those topics in many books, podcasts, and videos. Mike lives with his wife, Kim, and their two daughters, Brooklyn and Maya; runs long distances; and plays soccer with other middle-aged men whose best days are long behind them.

Find ways to watch *Time of Grace* with Pastor Mike by scanning this code.

OTHER BOOKS BY MIKE

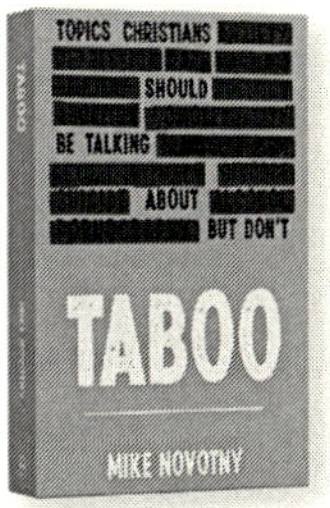

Taboo
Topics Christians Should Be Talking About but Don't

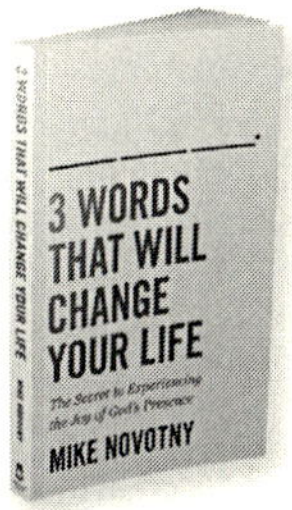

3 Words That Will Change Your Life
The Secret to Experiencing the Joy of God's Presence

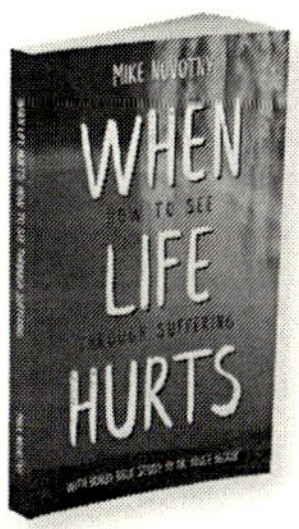

When Life Hurts
How to See Through Suffering

You Know God Loves You, Right?

Find these books and more by scanning the code or visiting timeofgrace.store.

ABOUT TIME OF GRACE

Time of Grace is for people who are experiencing the highest of highs or have hit rock bottom or are anywhere in between. That's because through Time of Grace, you will be reminded that the One who can help you in your life, the God of forgiveness and grace and mercy, is not far away. He is right here with you. GOD is here! He will help you on your spiritual journey. Walk with us at timeofgrace.org.

To discover more, please visit timeofgrace.org or scan this code:

HELP SHARE GOD'S MESSAGE OF GRACE!

Every gift you give helps Time of Grace reach people around the world with the good news of Jesus. Your generosity and prayer support take the gospel of grace to others through our ministry outreach and help them experience a satisfied life as they see God all around them.

Give today at timeofgrace.org/give,
by calling 800.661.3311.
or by scanning the code below.

Thank you!